'**T**his question is for £32,000.

"Which pop singer sang the theme of  *The Golden Gun?*"

A. Sheena Easton
B. Shirley Bassey
C. Lulu
D. Tom Jones

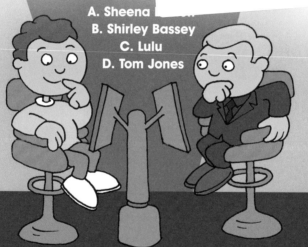

You don't have to answer this one, it's entirely up to you, you have already got £16,000 and you have used up your lifelines.'

'I think I'm going to go for it. My immediate thought was Tom Jones, but that's because my mum loves him and thinks he's great. But I feel pretty sure it's Shirley Bassey. I can almost hear her sing it. You are only on the programme once. So what the heck!'

'You said you would be delighted with £8,000. That would pay for your father's operation. Well you have got that and a lot more, so you don't really need to go on, but it's up to you.
It's your game.'

'I know, but a little bit more would be just fantastic. I think I will go for it: the answer is Shirley Bassey.'

'Final answer?'

'Yes'

'I'm so sorry, John. It's the wrong answer. The answer is Lulu!
John goes away with £1,000.'

'That money talks,
I'll not deny,
I heard it once,
It said goodbye.'

Anon.

There is something in all of us that wants that little bit more.

What is it about money that caused a learned man to say, 'The love of money is the root of all evil?' He also said, 'I have been rich and I have been poor, and I have learned in whatever state I am to be content.'

I wonder if that is really possible.
It sounds so attractive.
It is contentment that we are all
actually after. . .
but a bit more money would help!

Maybe this is one way to get it!

An Englishman an Irishman and a Scotsman attended the funeral of their friend.

As they lowered the coffin into the ground, the Englishman said,

'Oh, I owed Bill £10.' So he dropped a ten pound note on the top of the coffin, thus clearing his conscience.

The Irishman said, 'I also owed Bill £10.'

He put another £10 on top of the coffin.

His conscience was clear.

The Scotsman thought for a moment and said,

'I owed him £10 as well.'

So he took out his chequebook and wrote out a cheque for £30.

He put the cheque on top of the coffin and took the £20 change!

'Whoever loves money never has enough; whoever loves wealth is never satisfied with his income.'

— King Solomon

'Hapiness is not having what you want, it is wanting what you have.'

—Anon

We know that we need money in one form or another, but why does it cause us so much trouble and heartache as well as pleasure?

Money itself is of no value whatsoever apart from the value of a piece of metal or a bit of paper. Its value is in what it can obtain. It is the purchasing power that makes it so important to us. We need money in order to live, but so often it moves beyond that to controlling us.

One of the things that demonstrates our love affair with money is the National Lottery.

Every weekend in the UK, at least 30 million people buy a lottery ticket, knowing that they have almost no chance of winning. Why is the lottery so successful, and what does it show us about how most of us relate to money?

Does it appeal to our fear?

When the lottery was increased from once to twice a week, the vast majority of regulars began to play twice. Many people reported that they found themselves compelled to play more than they wanted to, not just because they wanted to win but out of fear that if they did not play it might have been the time that their number came up. So the addiction is created out of fear.

Does it appeal to our greed?

Since few of us ever have enough, the offer of something for almost nothing is too much to turn down. In a recent survey of people from all income brackets a questions was asked, 'If you could have more, how much would you need to be satisfied?' Almost everyone gave the same answer: about 25 per cent.

Does it appeal to our emptiness?

In a recent street poll in our area, people were asked which word most summed up their lives. The most popular word by far was the word empty. It is an interesting word because it presumes the possibility of being full. In other words, it expresses a common belief that somehow we are not meant to live like this, with a continual thirst for more.

If your life is empty you try to fill it. Most of us try holidays, homes, cars, and stuff, more stuff and even more stuff!

Have you ever found yourself in this circle of emotions?

I desire:

I see something. I realise that I do not have it. I believe that I would be better off if I did have it. I want it.

I dream:

I fix my mind and my imagination on the desired object. I long for it. I must have. I will have it. I have it.

I delight:

I am excited by my new purchase, which brings me great pleasure and joy. I feel good about what I have and I enjoy the admiration of others.

I am disappointed:

My new possession loses its charm and the excitement fades as I discover that it is only an object, a bit of stuff. It is nice, but there is now something better on the market.

I am discontented:

I look around for something else.

(Can you imagine how frustrating that must be if it occurs at the time you have to start paying for your 'don't pay now, have interest free credit for one year' purchase!)

I desire:. . . Whoops, haven't I been here before? Yes, but this is different!

Over the last few years, I have met large numbers of young people who have gone to Africa on short trips of a few weeks or months.

On their return, I have asked them, 'What most struck you about the people?'

The most common answer has been, 'The poverty and the joy.'
So then I ask, 'What struck you when you came back?'

The most common answer has been, 'The material abundance and the heavy, joyless atmosphere.'

In the Western world, our society is deeply influenced by

Hedonism –   the love of pleasure

Narcissism –   the love of self

Materialism – the love of stuff

And all these are wrapped up in consumerism which has a powerful influence on us all.

The desire to have more is driven by the consumer spirit. This itself is stirred up and driven by the power of advertising which affects all of us. If advertising were only informing, it could be seen as a service, but behind it are powerful persuaders also driven by the pursuit of money.

Consider the ideas behind advertising.

1. The motivation

What is the driving force behind advertising . . .

a). A concern for our welfare?

b). A loving desire to meet our needs?
Or
c). The creation of artificial needs?

How many of us never think of buying something until we either see it advertised or owned by someone else?

2. The message

The underlying assumptions are that:

● Things will satisfy. The quality of our life is increased by the quantity and quality of our possessions. Strange how the rich know that this is not true but we don't believe them.

● Acceptance and love are related to the ownership of the right things.

● Success is the greatest goal, and material possessions are a sign of success.

● Relationships are built on outward appearance. The rich, suave man driving the right car gets the girl! The girl in the fragrant perfume gets her man.

3. The method

Have you noticed what advertising appeals to?

It is to our:
● Vulnerability
We have an inbuilt craving for more.
Of course we do. If what we have does not satisfy, we must need more.

● Anxiety
We feel that we would be more secure if we owned the right stuff.

● The desire for sexual fulfilment

Most advertising carries the promise of sexual fulfilment. If you buy the right car or use the right fragrance, sexual conquest is a certainty and relationship is idyllic.

● Pride

We want others to think well of us and to look up to us and we are told that having the right things will help.

Maybe we need to see advertising for what it is. If you come to terms with its underlying motivation, its hidden message and the subtle method, you are armed to deal with the powerful invader in your life.

Important lesson: try talking back to TV ads, questioning their truthfulness. Get free of being pushed around by the uninvited salesman encased in your living room!

As we get lured by advertising and seduced by consumerism, so many find themselves caught in the debt trap.

In a recent BBC programme, it was reported that, 'the British public is in the grip of a new disease. According to the experts we've caught luxury fever.'

'In Britain, we now owe a total of £905,782,000,000 – that is £15,300 debt for every man, woman and child in the country.'

Another report says that in the UK today:

● The Citizens' Advice Bureau receives 1 million debt inquiries in a year.

● The level of secured debt has risen by 70 per cent in five years.

● Money owed on overdrafts is £5.7 billion.

● Money owed on personal loans is £41 billion.

● Money owed on credit cards is £21 billion.

There are few things in life worse than being trapped by debt. It is like being in a pit with vertical sides. Every time you make an effort to get out, you fall back again.

The easy availability of credit cards and the extent of credit allowed make disaster all the more likely, as it seems so easy and painless at the time.

All around my local
post office this year
were posters asking
the question,
'Why wait for what
you want?'

WHY WAIT FOR WHAT YOU WANT?

There was a time when
people paid cash
for what they bought and didn't buy it unless
they could afford it.

If those are the influences from the outside,
there are equally loud voices coming from
within us.

There are four basic needs in every human being. Because these
remain substantially unfulfilled in most of us, we look to money and
stuff to meet these needs.

They are:

Security

There are certain basic physical elements of life that everyone needs in order to survive. These are food and water, clothing and shelter. The need for security is a concern that we have these things now and in the future. We want to know that everything will be OK.

Can money buy security? If so, how much do you need?

Significance

In the Western world, we have come to believe that a sense of worth is given to us by other people and is related to what we have, what we wear, where we live, etc.

A Rolls Royce goes by and everyone looks to see who is in it. An old Mini Metro goes by and nobody cares!

Can money buy significance?

Status

A sense of value is what we all crave. It is often assumed that our position in life is dependent on our wealth. The rich are to be envied, admired and given celebrity status. The poor receive no such attention.

The Sunday Times have yet to produce
'The Poor List' of the top 1,000 poorest people in Britain.

Can money buy status or a sense of value?

Satisfaction

Satisfaction is the pursuit of happiness. This has something to do with enjoying life. It is comes from owning things, going places and doing what you please.

Can money buy satisfaction and happiness?

These are very real inner needs, that have to be met.

Money appears to buy fulfilment but it fails miserably in every area. That is the problem and only the rich fully know this to be true.

It is not the fault of money. It is this way because money was never intended to provide security, significance, value or happiness. They come from somewhere, or rather someone else. It is that simple.

**'Do You Really Think I'm a Material Girl? I'm not.
I don't need money. I need Love.'** Madonna.

The strange thing about money is that it has a light side and a dark side. We all aspire to the one but find ourselves strangely drawn into the other.

The light side of money

Money has huge potential for good. There can be great benefits in being rich, provided that your money does not own you and that you have a big and generous heart.

Money has the ability to express love and kindness. Money can be used to bring help and joy to so many people in so many ways when it is given generously and sacrificially and without control.

Money can provide for the needs of those who are suffering and living with insufficient provision for life.

Here is what one child-sponsoring agency, Compassion, has to say, 'You can sponsor a child for £18 a month – that is about 60p a day to support one child in need. It's extraordinary what just a small amount will do in the developing world. The amount of difference you can bring about with that small investment is just amazing!' 60p brings hope to one child.

Money can provide us with a great deal of pleasure and fun and enable us to enjoy the world in which we live.

The Dark Side of Money

Money is neutral, but behind money is a power. The power of
materialism is dark. It is the power behind pornography, prostitution,
political corruption, drugs, poverty, ecological mismanagement,
war and political upheaval, as well as personal debt. Its voices are
familiar.

It is persistent in its demands:
'You must possess more, get a bigger mortgage, work harder,
longer hours, sacrifice family, friends and health, always go for
bigger and better.'

It is cunning in its deception:
'Never let on what you earn,
how much you own and
certainly never be open about
your debts. Keep a bit away
from your spouse. After all you
are entitled to a bit of
independence and freedom.'

It is subtle in its seduction:
'Get more and you will be
happy, be loved more,
sexually fulfilled and secure for
life. A bigger house and a
better car will certainly make
you happier.'

In accepting its message, we get everything out of perspective. We lose sight of the difference between essential and luxury because the media will not allow us that distinction.

An Arab proverb says...

'I cried because I had no socks, until I met a man who had no feet.'

Is there anywhere we could look to sort this all out?

My suggestion may seem strange to some, but you maybe surprised at what you find.

The Bible is a book that gives a remarkably perceptive view of life: it takes us beyond the superficial to see what is really going on, and best of all it offers us hope. But here is a word of warning: the answers may be more radical and far-reaching than most of us are prepared for.

Here are three key principles:

● If you stack up material stuff in your life, owning more and more, saving more and more, it will always be steadily eaten away, fade away and lose its attraction. If you use your money for things of lasting value, i.e. helping others, it is an investment that will produce a good return for everyone and ultimately be far more satisfying.

● If God is not boss in your life (either because you do not believe in him or because to accept this sounds like a restrictive form of living) then money will actually become your master. In fact, if you take a closer look you will find it already makes all your decisions for you, i.e. which house you live in, what you own, where you holiday.

These, and other decisions in life, will be determined by the amount or lack of money you have. In other words, money is in control of you.

If God is boss, money becomes your servant.

You cannot have two bosses.

● Whether you have a lot or a little, you will never be free of anxiety or worry. You will always be concerned to sustain what you have and feel that it all depends on you. You will never feel completely free or feel at peace about the future.

● If you believe that this world is all there is, then you will be concerned to 'eat, drink and be merry' and that takes as much stuff as possible.

The sense of vulnerability, the sense of being controlled, and the sense of anxiety and drive that dominates so many people was never intended to be our experience.

A child may be given pocket money to learn responsibility and be able to buy things for himself, but the parent has ultimate responsibility for the provision of the child's basic needs and pleasure.

In the same way, this is how it is meant to be with us. It was always intended that God would parent us and be the one responsible, but when we turn our back on God, we have to face the consequences.

We should be living lives of contentment, free from worry, but it is not so.

I realise that all this sounds radical in today's society, but it was these simple truths that Jesus taught in order to show people that there is another way to live.

Not only did he teach it, but he also made it possible to rediscover what has been lost. Jesus did all that was necessary to restore our relationship so that we could come to know God as `Dad.'

If you come to know God in this way, you can learn to live free of the fear that what you need will all run out, because he will look after you. You may have a lot or a little, either way you will have enough. You can even begin to give away what you have to those who have less.

It is actually true that, 'it is more fun and more satisfying to give than to receive.'

When God is in charge of your life, money becomes your servant. It no longer controls you, but you can do with it as you choose. You no longer need to buy significance, status and security, as they come from another source.

Since all of these needs are met by knowing God, you are then free to give other people enormous pleasure by living on the light side. The influences on the outside remain unchanged, but the new strength from within lessens the vulnerability.

Think about it. It sounds good and it might actually work!

The words of a great teacher:

'Keep yourself free from the love of money.
For he has said, "I will never leave you or forsake you."'

It is much easier to experience the first part of this statement if you come to experience the second.

Helpful hints to living free from money-pressure

1. Be aware of where you are in the world economy. If you live in the West, with running water in your house and have at least one change of clothes, plus at least two meals a day, you number amongst the world's rich.

Why go in pursuit of more and more, when you are already rich? Try helping others.

2. **Be grateful** for what you have instead of being obsessed with what you don't have. Golden rule: look down, not up! Make a habit of looking at people with less, rather than looking at people with more. Find an opportunity every day to be thankful.

3. Fix your standards

The government is always promising to raise our standards of living, as if that is what we all need. It is true that many are struggling and need help, but nobody ever feels they have enough, so at some point call a halt and choose to be satisfied.

4. Be a giver

Find opportunities to give away to others. The Bible encourages us to discipline ourselves to give away a percentage (many go for 10 per cent) of our income. I have never met anyone who has done that and subsequently been worse off. You discover a new form of maths: giving away produces more.

Why not try it?

5. Budget carefully

If you do not budget, you will always be out of control. Careful budgeting keeps you from debt and enables you to plan ahead for holidays, etc.

Most of us do not know how to do this, so if you have never done it, get help from someone who has.

6. Clear debt

Do everything you can to get debt free. Debt causes worry, anxiety and often depression. If you are in debt, work out a plan to get out over a period of time; cut back on everything to get level again.

7. Keep free

It's a good rule in life to decide to never get overdrawn at the bank, and never to use credit cards if you don't have the money to pay. It is better to wait for what you want and then to have the joy of owning it, than to be in debt.

If you are overdrawn, the only people who will be helpful will be the bank, so they won't discourage you. Having an overdraft is borrowing someone else's money and is another form of debt.

8. Only buy what you can pay for. Resist the temptation to borrow or to buy with plastic when you know you do not have the money. Save and buy is far more rewarding.

If this is a major problem **try taking a pair of scissors to your plastic cards.** Go right away and cut up all your cards unless you are in control.

It works wonders.

9. Aim for simplicity

More stuff means more and more concerns, and simplicity means freedom. Look at ways to simplify your life. Give away everything that you don't use. Only buy what you need. Clear away clutter and you will be amazed how good it feels.

Key questions to ask:

Do I want it?

Do I need it?

Can I afford it?

10. Trust God with your life

Let him be your dad. He wants to look after you materially as well as spiritually. Jesus came to make that possible. When you understand what Jesus has done for you, the way home is open for you.

There is nothing more exciting than coming to know him.
That is the way to be free from continual anxiety and to have real joy and peace.

Where do we go from here?

If you want to make this discovery for yourself, I suggest you:

● Look on the website www.makingsenseoflife.com

● Talk to a Christian friend.

● Find a place where you can discuss these things further
(such as an Alpha Course *www.alphacourse.org,* Christianity Explored
www.christianityexplored, or The Y Course *www.premieronline.co.uk*).

First published 2004 by Authentic Media, 9 Holdom Avenue, Bletchley, Milton Keynes, Bucks, MK1 1QR, UK and
PO Box 1047, Waynesboro, GA 30830-2047, USA.

08 07 06 05 04 7 6 5 4 3 1

British Library Cataloguing in Publication Data
A catalogue record for this book is available from the British Library.

1-86024-470-X

Illustrated by Alan Birch